MORE POEMS

A. E. HOUSMAN

July 1926

From a drawing by Francis Dodd

MORE POEMS

by

A. E. HOUSMAN

JONATHAN CAPE
THIRTY BEDFORD SQUARE
LONDON

FIRST PUBLISHED 1936

JONATHAN CAPE LTD.   30 BEDFORD SQUARE, LONDON
AND 91 WELLINGTON STREET WEST, TORONTO

PRINTED IN GREAT BRITAIN IN THE CITY OF OXFORD
AT THE ALDEN PRESS
PAPER MADE BY GROSVENOR, CHATER & CO. LTD.
BOUND BY A. W. BAIN & CO. LTD.

PREFACE

THIS final selection of A. E. Housman's poems is published by his permission, not by his wish. His instructions, allowing them to appear, while committing other material to a less fortunate fate, were as follows:

> 'I direct my brother, Laurence Housman, to destroy all my prose manuscripts in whatever language, and I permit him but do not enjoin him to select from my verse manuscript writing, and to publish, any poems which appear to him to be completed and to be not inferior to the average of my published poems; and I direct him to destroy all other poems and fragments of verse.'

The responsibility which has thus been laid on me is of a double character; for while I am anxious to include nothing that can do hurt to my brother's literary reputation, I am most reluctant to deprive his lovers of any poems, however minor in character, which are not inferior to others – also minor in character – which have already been published.

So far as he himself was concerned, he had no desire to add to the two selections he had already made, either from the poems then left out, or from the few which were written subsequently. But consideration for the wishes of others became increasingly apparent in his last years; and since he has made me the instrument of that consideration, I feel bound to give it as sympathetic an interpretation as possible.

My main difficulty has been this: that while I would naturally wish to give any poem of minor merit the benefit of the doubt, and am therefore inclined to err on

7

the side of leniency, I know well that his own decision would be more likely to err on the side of severity. But since in only one case has he crossed out a finished poem with the written comment 'not good', it would seem that he intended to leave all the rest freely to my own judgment – average merit and completeness being the limiting conditions.

Several of these poems, as were some of *Last Poems* also, are of *Shropshire Lad* date, and though the name of 'Terence', which he chose for the imaginary writer of the poems, does not reappear, it is evident that a good many, especially those from page 27 to page 48, belong to the Terence series, and through the mouth of that invented character express, sometimes contradictorily, the turbulent and changing moods of troubled youth. In an autobiographical note supplied to a French writer, 'The *Shropshire Lad*', my brother explained, 'is an imaginary character, with something of my temper and view of life. Very little in the book is biographical'.

In the present volume only the introductory poem, the one bearing initials for title, and one or two toward the end are directly personal. The earlier group above referred to are poems of a time of life which the author had long passed when he wrote them; but none the less they are characteristic of the lively sympathy which, in the words of the opening poem of this collection, he had for 'all ill-treated fellows', and more especially for the young. He would have liked 'the laws of God and man' to be kinder than they are; and a great deal of the anger and bitterness of his verse is due to the fact that they are so much the other way.

Several of these poems were paged and numbered for inclusion in *Last Poems*, and one of them (No. XLV) was actually printed; but as the author had previously left out from the planned sequence of *A Shropshire Lad*, for reasons which were merely selective, verses which afterwards appeared in *Last Poems*, I have not taken later omissions to mean final rejection.

The poem 'For my funeral' was written in 1925, and was, as shown in the list of dated poems given at the end of this volume, the last to have its date recorded. Only the poems named in this list have been dated by the author; but from their place of sequence in a set of four closely-filled notebooks, the dates of a good many other poems can be inferred. These notebooks I am under orders to destroy; but before doing so I intend to make a paged list of their contents, which will give a fairly accurate chronology of most of the published poems.

It may be some consolation to those who regret this order for destruction, to know that there are no fragments or unfinished poems of outstanding quality. A few beautiful phrases, sometimes single verses, will have to go. One or two which, in spite of extreme brevity, seem to stand on their own, I have felt justified in retaining. The rest is mainly work-shop material – fragmentary, but interesting as showing the author's process of composition – his many alterations of phrase or rhyme before finding the one which best satisfied him. From these I am fortunately able to preserve just one example of alternative readings – a poem of which there are two complete variants (Nos. x and xi), with no indication as to which of the two the author preferred; and though I have a slight preference myself, I am not so confident of my judgment being right as to deny to others the interest and pleasure of making their own choice.

In choosing between other variant readings limited to single lines, words, or phrases, and also in making the selection which here follows, I have been greatly helped by the kind services and wise counsel of three of my

9

brother's contemporaries of Trinity and King's College, Cambridge: Professor G. M. Trevelyan, o.m., Mr. Andrew Gow, and Mr. F. L. Lucas; and though they are not to be held finally responsible for what has here been included, and what left out, their good advice – for which I am most grateful – has had a not inconsiderable influence on the selection as it now stands.

I have also to thank the President and Fellows of St. John's College, Oxford, for their kind permission to reproduce the Francis Dodd drawing which forms the frontispiece, and which in my view is the best portrait of my brother that has ever been done.

L.H.

CONTENTS

MORE POEMS

They say my verse is sad: no wonder;
  Its narrow measure spans
Tears of eternity, and sorrow,
  Not mine, but man's.

This is for all ill-treated fellows
  Unborn and unbegot,
For them to read when they're in trouble
  And I am not.

EASTER HYMN

If in that Syrian garden, ages slain,
You sleep, and know not you are dead in vain,
Nor even in dreams behold how dark and bright
Ascends in smoke and fire by day and night
The hate you died to quench and could but fan,
Sleep well and see no morning, son of man.

But if, the grave rent and the stone rolled by,
At the right hand of majesty on high
You sit, and sitting so remember yet
Your tears, your agony and bloody sweat,
Your cross and passion and the life you gave,
Bow hither out of heaven and see and save.

When Israel out of Egypt came,
   Safe in the sea they trod;
By day in cloud, by night in flame,
   Went on before them God.

He brought them with a stretched out hand
   Dry-footed through the foam,
Past sword and famine, rock and sand,
   Lust and rebellion, home.

I never over Horeb heard
   The blast of advent blow;
No fire-faced prophet brought me word
   Which way behoved me go.

Ascended is the cloudy flame,
   The mount of thunder dumb;
The tokens that to Israel came,
   To me they have not come.

I see the country far away
   Where I shall never stand;
The heart goes where no footstep may
   Into the promised land.

The realm I look upon and die
   Another man will own;
He shall attain the heaven that I
   Perish and have not known.

But I will go where they are hid
   That never were begot,
To my inheritance amid
   The nation that is not,

Where mixed with me the sandstorms drift,
    And nerve and heart and brain
Are ashes for the air to lift
    And lightly shower again.

For these of old the trader
   Unpearled the Indian seas,
The nations of the nadir
   Were diamondless for these;

A people prone and haggard
   Beheld their lightnings hurled:
All round, like Sinai, staggered
   The sceptre-shaken world.

But now their coins are tarnished,
   Their towers decayed away,
Their kingdom swept and garnished
   For haler kings than they;

Their arms the rust hath eaten,
   Their statutes none regard:
Arabia shall not sweeten
   Their dust, with all her nard.

They cease from long vexation,
   Their nights, their days are done,
The pale, the perished nation
   That never see the sun;

From the old deep-dusted annals
   The years erase their tale,
And round them race the channels
   That take no second sail.

THE SAGE TO THE YOUNG MAN

O youth whose heart is right,
  Whose loins are girt to gain
The hell-defended height
  Where Virtue beckons plain;

Who seest the stark array
  And hast not stayed to count
But singly wilt assay
  The many-cannoned mount:

Well is thy war begun;
  Endure, be strong and strive;
But think not, O my son,
  To save thy soul alive.

Wilt thou be true and just
  And clean and kind and brave?
Well; but for all thou dost,
  Be sure it shall not save.

Thou, when the night falls deep,
  Thou, though the mount be won,
High heart, thou shalt but sleep
  The sleep denied to none.

Others, or ever thou,
  To scale those heights were sworn;
And some achieved, but now
  They never see the morn.

How shouldst thou keep the prize?
  Thou wast not born for aye.
Content thee if thine eyes
  Behold it in thy day.

O youth that wilt attain,
  On, for thine hour is short.
It may be thou shalt gain
  The hell-defended fort.

V

DIFFUGERE NIVES

Horace: Odes iv 7

The snows are fled away, leaves on the shaws
  And grasses in the mead renew their birth,
The river to the river-bed withdraws,
  And altered is the fashion of the earth.

The Nymphs and Graces three put off their fear
  And unapparelled in the woodland play.
The swift hour and the brief prime of the year
  Say to the soul, *Thou wast not born for aye.*

Thaw follows frost; hard on the heel of spring
  Treads summer sure to die, for hard on hers
Comes autumn with his apples scattering;
  Then back to wintertide, when nothing stirs.

But oh, whate'er the sky-led seasons mar,
  Moon upon moon rebuilds it with her beams;
Come we where Tullus and where Ancus are
  And good Aeneas, we are dust and dreams.

Torquatus, if the gods in heaven shall add
  The morrow to the day, what tongue has told?
Feast then thy heart, for what thy heart has had
  The fingers of no heir will ever hold.

When thou descendest once the shades among,
  The stern assize and equal judgment o'er,
Not thy long lineage nor thy golden tongue,
  No, nor thy righteousness, shall friend thee more.

21

Night holds Hippolytus the pure of stain,
    Diana steads him nothing, he must stay;
And Theseus leaves Pirithous in the chain
    The love of comrades cannot take away.

I to my perils
  Of cheat and charmer
  Came clad in armour
    By stars benign.
Hope lies to mortals
  And most believe her,
  But man's deceiver
    Was never mine.

The thoughts of others
  Were light and fleeting,
  Of lovers' meeting
    Or luck or fame.
Mine were of trouble,
  And mine were steady,
  So I was ready
    When trouble came.

Stars, I have seen them fall,
  But when they drop and die
No star is lost at all
  From all the star-sown sky.
The toil of all that be
  Helps not the primal fault;
It rains into the sea,
  And still the sea is salt.

Give me a land of boughs in leaf,
   A land of trees that stand;
Where trees are fallen, there is grief;
   I love no leafless land.

Alas, the country whence I fare,
   It is where I would stay;
And where I would not, it is there
   That I shall be for aye.

And one remembers and forgets,
   But 'tis not found again,
Not though they hale in crimsoned nets
   The sunset from the main.

When green buds hang in the elm like dust
  And sprinkle the lime like rain,
Forth I wander, forth I must,
  And drink of life again.

Forth I must by hedgerow bower
  To look at the leaves uncurled,
And stand in fields where cuckoo flowers
  Are lying about the world.

The weeping Pleiads wester,
  And the moon is under seas;
From bourn to bourn of midnight
  Far sighs the rainy breeze:

It sighs from a lost country
  To a land I have not known;
The weeping Pleiads wester,
  And I lie down alone.

The rainy Pleiads wester,
    Orion plunges prone,
The stroke of midnight ceases
    And I lie down alone.

The rainy Pleiads wester
    And seek beyond the sea
The head that I shall dream of
    That will not dream of me.

I promise nothing: friends will part;
   All things may end, for all began;
And truth and singleness of heart
   Are mortal even as is man.

But this unlucky love should last
   When answered passions thin to air;
Eternal fate so deep has cast
   Its sure foundation of despair.

I lay me down and slumber
  And every morn revive.
Whose is the night-long breathing
  That keeps me man alive?

When I was off to dreamland
  And left my limbs forgot,
Who stayed at home to mind them,
  And breathed when I did not?

I waste my time in talking,
  No heed at all takes he,
My kind and foolish comrade
  That breathes all night for me.

The farms of home lie lost in even,
  I see far off the steeple stand;
West and away from here to heaven
    Still is the land.

There if I go no girl will greet me,
  No comrade hollo from the hill,
No dog run down the yard to meet me:
    The land is still.

The land is still by farm and steeple,
  And still for me the land may stay:
There I was friends with perished people,
  And there lie they.

XV

Tarry delight, so seldom met,
  So sure to perish, tarry still;
Forbear to cease or languish yet,
  Though soon you must and will.

By Sestos town, in Hero's tower,
  On Hero's heart Leander lies;
The signal torch has burned its hour
  And sputters as it dies.

Beneath him, in the nighted firth,
  Between two continents complain
The seas he swam from earth to earth
  And he must swim again.

How clear, how lovely bright,
How beautiful to sight
    Those beams of morning play;
How heaven laughs out with glee
Where, like a bird set free,
Up from the eastern sea
    Soars the delightful day.

To-day I shall be strong,
No more shall yield to wrong,
    Shall squander life no more;
Days lost, I know not how,
I shall retrieve them now;
Now I shall keep the vow
    I never kept before.

    .   .   .   .   .

Ensanguining the skies
How heavily it dies
    Into the west away;
Past touch and sight and sound
Not further to be found
How hopeless underground
    Falls the remorseful day.

Bells in tower at evening toll,
And the day forsakes the soul;
Soon will evening's self be gone
And the whispering night come on.

Blame not thou the blinded light
Nor the whisper of the night:
Though the whispering night were still,
Yet the heart would counsel ill.

Delight it is in youth and May
   To see the morn arise,
And more delight to look all day
   A lover in the eyes.
Oh maiden, let your distaff be,
And pace the flowery meads with me,
   And I will tell you lies.

'Tis blithe to see the sunshine fail,
   And hear the land grow still,
And listen till the nightingale
   Is heard beneath the hill.
Oh follow me where she is flown
Into the leafy woods alone,
   And I will work you ill.

The mill-stream, now that noises cease,
Is all that does not hold its peace;
Under the bridge it murmurs by,
And here are night and hell and I.

Who made the world I cannot tell;
'Tis made, and here am I in hell.
My hand, though now my knuckles bleed,
I never soiled with such a deed.

And so, no doubt, in time gone by,
Some have suffered more than I,
Who only spend the night alone
And strike my fist upon the stone.

Like mine the veins of these that slumber
   Leapt once with dancing fires divine;
The blood of all this noteless number
   Ran red like mine.

How still, with every pulse in station,
   Frost in the founts that used to leap,
The put-to-death, the perished nation
   How sound they sleep!

These too, these veins which life convulses,
   Wait but a while, shall cease to bound;
I with the ice in all my pulses
   Shall sleep as sound.

The world goes none the lamer,
  For ought that I can see,
Because this cursed trouble
  Has struck my days and me.

The stars of heaven are steady,
  The founded hills remain,
Though I to earth and darkness
  Return in blood and pain.

Farewell to all belongings
  I won or bought or stole;
Farewell, my lusty carcase,
  Farewell, my aery soul.

Oh worse remains for others,
  And worse to fear had I
Than here at four-and-twenty
  To lay me down and die.

Ho, everyone that thirsteth
  And hath the price to give,
Come to the stolen waters,
  Drink and your soul shall live.

Come to the stolen waters,
  And leap the guarded pale,
And pull the flower in season
  Before desire shall fail.

It shall not last for ever,
  No more than earth and skies;
But he that drinks in season
  Shall live before he dies.

June suns, you cannot store them
  To warm the winter's cold,
The lad that hopes for heaven
  Shall fill his mouth with mould.

Crossing alone the nighted ferry
　　With the one coin for fee,
Whom, on the wharf of Lethe waiting,
　　Count you to find? Not me.

The brisk fond lackey to fetch and carry,
　　The true, sick-hearted slave,
Expect him not in the just city
　　And free land of the grave.

Stone, steel, dominions pass,
  Faith too, no wonder;
So leave alone the grass
  That I am under.
All knots that lovers tie
  Are tied to sever;
Here shall your sweet-heart lie,
  Untrue for ever.

XXV

Yon fire that frets the eastern sky
    Leads back my day of birth;
The far, wide-wandered hour when I
    Came crying upon earth.

Then came I crying, and to-day,
    With heavier cause to plain,
Depart I into death away,
    Not to be born again.

Good creatures, do you love your lives
  And have you ears for sense?
Here is a knife like other knives,
  That cost me eighteen pence.

I need but stick it in my heart
  And down will come the sky,
And earth's foundations will depart
  And all you folk will die.

XXVII

To stand up straight and tread the turning mill,
To lie flat and know nothing and be still,
Are the two trades of man; and which is worse
I know not, but I know that both are ill.

He, standing hushed, a pace or two apart,
  Among the bluebells of the listless plain,
Thinks, and remembers how he cleansed his heart
  And washed his hands in innocence in vain.

From the wash the laundress sends
My collars home with ravelled ends;
I must fit, now these are frayed,
My neck with new ones London-made.

Homespun collars, homespun hearts,
Wear to rags in foreign parts.
Mine at least's as good as done,
And I must get a London one.

Shake hands, we shall never be friends, all's over;
  I only vex you the more I try.
All's wrong that ever I've done or said,
And nought to help it in this dull head:
  Shake hands, here's luck, good-bye.

But if you come to a road where danger
  Or guilt or anguish or shame's to share,
Be good to the lad that loves you true
And the soul that was born to die for you,
  And whistle and I'll be there.

Because I liked you better
    Than suits a man to say,
It irked you, and I promised
    To throw the thought away.

To put the world between us
    We parted, stiff and dry;
'Good-bye', said you, 'forget me.'
    'I will, no fear', said I.

If here, where clover whitens
    The dead man's knoll, you pass,
And no tall flower to meet you
    Starts in the trefoiled grass,

Halt by the headstone naming
    The heart no longer stirred,
And say the lad that loved you
    Was one that kept his word.

With seed the sowers scatter
    The furrows as they go;
Poor lads, 'tis little matter
    How many sorts they sow,
    For only one will grow.

The charlock on the fallow
    Will take the traveller's eyes,
And gild the ploughland sallow
    With flowers before it dies,
    But twice 'twill not arise.

The stinging nettle only
    Will still be found to stand:
The numberless, the lonely,
    The thronger of the land,
    The leaf that hurts the hand.

It thrives, come sun, come showers,
    Blow east, blow west, it springs;
It peoples towns, and towers
    Above the courts of Kings,
    And touch it and it stings.

On forelands high in heaven,
   'Tis many a year gone by,
Amidst the fall of even
   Would stand my friends and I.
Before our foolish faces
   Lay lands we did not see;
Our eyes were in the places
   Where we shall never be.

Oh, the pearl seas are yonder,
   The gold and amber shore;
Shires where the girls are fonder,
   Towns where the pots hold more.
And here fret we and moulder
   By grange and rick and shed
And every moon are older,
   And soon we shall be dead.

Heigho, 'twas true and pity;
   But there we lads must stay.
Troy was a steepled city,
   But Troy was far away.
And round we turned lamenting
   To homes we longed to leave,
And silent hills indenting
   The orange band of eve.

I see the air benighted
   And all the dusking dales,
And lamps in England lighted,
   And evening wrecked in Wales;
And starry darkness paces
   The roads from sea to sea,
And blots the foolish faces
   Of my poor friends and me.

Young is the blood that yonder
    Strides out the dusty mile,
And breasts the hillside highway
    And whistles loud the while,
    And vaults the stile.

On miry meads in winter
    The football sprung and fell;
May stuck the land with wickets:
    For all the eye could tell,
    The world went well.

Yet well, God knows, it went not,
    God knows it went awry;
For me, one flowery Maytime,
    It went so ill that I
    Designed to die.

And if so long I carry
    The lot that season marred,
'Tis that the sons of Adam
    Are not so evil-starred
    As they are hard.

Yet flesh, now too, has thorn-pricks,
    And shoulders carry care,
Even as in other seasons,
    When I and not my heir
    Was young and there.

Young is the blood that yonder
    Succeeds to rick and fold,
Fresh are the form and favour,
    And new the minted mould:
    The thoughts are old.

Half way, for one commandment broken,
  The woman made her endless halt,
And she to-day, a glittering token,
  Stands in the wilderness of salt.
Behind, the vats of judgment brewing
  Thundered, and thick the brimstone snowed;
He to the hill of his undoing
  Pursued his road.

Here dead lie we because we did not choose
    To live and shame the land from which we sprung.
Life, to be sure, is nothing much to lose;
    But young men think it is, and we were young.

I did not lose my heart in summer's even,
  When roses to the moonrise burst apart:
When plumes were under heel and lead was flying,
  In blood and smoke and flame I lost my heart.

I lost it to a soldier and a foeman,
  A chap that did not kill me, but he tried;
That took the sabre straight and took it striking,
  And laughed and kissed his hand to me and died.

By shores and woods and steeples
   Rejoicing hearts receive
Poured on a hundred peoples
   The far-shed alms of eve.

Her hands are filled with slumber
   For world-wide labourers worn;
Yet those are more in number
   That know her not from morn.

Now who sees night for ever,
   He sees no happier sight:
Night and no moon and never
   A star upon the night.

My dreams are of a field afar
   And blood and smoke and shot.
There in their graves my comrades are,
   In my grave I am not.

I too was taught the trade of man
   And spelt the lesson plain;
But they, when I forgot and ran,
   Remembered and remain.

Farewell to a name and a number,
　Recalled again
To darkness and silence and slumber
　In blood and pain.

So ceases and turns to the thing
　He was born to be
A soldier cheap to the King
　And dear to me.

So smothers in blood the burning
　And flaming flight
Of valour and truth, returning
　To dust and night.

He looked at me with eyes I thought
    I was not like to find;
The voice he begged for pence with brought
    Another man to mind.

Oh, no, lad, never touch your cap;
    It is not my half-crown;
You have it from a better chap
    That long ago lay down.

Turn east and over Thames to Kent
    And come to the sea's brim,
And find his everlasting tent
    And touch your cap to him.

A. J. J.

When he's returned I'll tell him – oh,
　　Dear fellow, I forgot:
Time was you would have cared to know,
　　But now it matters not.

I mourn you, and you heed not how;
　　Unsaid the word must stay;
Last month was time enough, but now
　　The news must keep for aye.

Oh, many a month before I learn
　　Will find me starting still
And listening, as the days return,
　　For him that never will.

Strange, strange to think his blood is cold
　　And mine flows easy on;
And that straight look, that heart of gold,
　　That grace, that manhood gone.

The word unsaid will stay unsaid
　　Though there was much to say;
Last month was time enough: he's dead,
　　The news must keep for aye.

I wake from dreams and turning
  My vision on the height
I scan the beacons burning
  About the fields of night.

Each in its steadfast station
  In flaming heaven they flare;
They sign with conflagration
  The empty moors of air.

The signal-fires of warning
  They blaze, but none regard;
And on through night to morning
  The world runs ruinward.

Far known to sea and shore,
  Foursquare and founded well,
A thousand years it bore,
  And then the belfry fell.
      The steersman of Triest
      Looked where his mark should be,
      But empty was the west
      And Venice under sea.

From dusty wreck dispersed
  Its stature mounts amain;
On surer foot than first
  The belfry stands again.
      At to-fall of the day
      Again its curfew tolls
      And burdens far away
      The green and sanguine shoals.

It looks to north and south,
  It looks to east and west;
It guides to Lido mouth
  The steersman of Triest.
      Andrea, fare you well;
      Venice farewell to thee.
      The tower that stood and fell
      Is not rebuilt in me.

Smooth between sea and land
Is laid the yellow sand,
And here through summer days
The seed of Adam plays.

Here the child comes to found
His unremaining mound,
And the grown lad to score
Two names upon the shore.

Here, on the level sand,
Between the sea and land,
What shall I build or write
Against the fall of night?

Tell me of runes to grave
That hold the bursting wave,
Or bastions to design
For longer date than mine.

Shall it be Troy or Rome
I fence against the foam,
Or my own name, to stay
When I depart for aye?

Nothing: too near at hand,
Planing the figured sand,
Effacing clean and fast
Cities not built to last
And charms devised in vain,
Pours the confounding main.

THE LAND OF BISCAY

Sons of landsmen, sons of seamen,
  hear the tale of grief and me,
Looking from the land of Biscay
  on the waters of the sea.

Looking from the land of Biscay
  over Ocean to the sky
On the far-beholding foreland
  paced at even grief and I.
There, as warm the west was burning
  and the east uncoloured cold,
Down the waterway of sunset
  drove to shore a ship of gold.
Gold of mast and gold of cordage,
  gold of sail to sight was she,
And she glassed her ensign golden
  in the waters of the sea.

Oh, said I, my friend and lover,
  take we now that ship and sail
Outward in the ebb of hues and
  steer upon the sunset trail;
Leave the night to fall behind us
  and the clouding counties leave:
Help for you and me is yonder,
  in the havens west of eve.

Under hill she neared the harbour,
  till the gazer could behold
On the golden deck the steersman
  standing at the helm of gold,

Man and ship and sky and water
    burning in a single flame;
And the mariner of Ocean
    he was calling as he came:
From the highway of the sunset
    he was shouting on the sea,
'Landsman of the land of Biscay,
    have you help for grief and me?'

When I heard I did not answer,
    I stood mute and shook my head:
Son of earth and son of Ocean,
    much we thought and nothing said.
Grief and I abode the nightfall;
    to the sunset grief and he
Turned them from the land of Biscay
    on the waters of the sea.

FOR MY FUNERAL

O thou that from thy mansion
   Through time and place to roam,
Dost send abroad thy children,
   And then dost call them home,

That men and tribes and nations
   And all thy hand hath made
May shelter them from sunshine
   In thine eternal shade:

We now to peace and darkness
   And earth and thee restore
Thy creature that thou madest
   And wilt cast forth no more.

ALTA QUIES

Good-night. Ensured release,
Imperishable peace,
    Have these for yours,
While earth's foundations stand
And sky and sea and land
    And heaven endures.

When earth's foundations flee,
Nor sky nor land nor sea
    At all is found.
Content you; let them burn,
It is not your concern:
    Sleep on, sleep sound.

DATED POEMS

DATED POEMS

THE following are the poems to which dates are given in the Author's note-books. All but two were published either in *A Shropshire Lad* or in *Last Poems*.

Once in the wind of morning: Sept. 1890
In Summer-time on Bredon: July 1891
Far in a western brookland: 1891-2
'Tis time, I think, by Wenlock Town: Feb. 1893
The weeping Pleiads wester: Feb. 1893
With Rue my Heart is laden: Aug. 1893
Farewell to barn and stack and tree: Aug. 1894
The Lad came to the door at night: Dec. 1894
When I was one-and-twenty: Jan. 1895
Wake: the silver dusk returning: Jan. 1895
Leave your home behind, lad: Jan. 1895
High the vanes of Shrewsbury gleam: Jan. 1895
On moonlit heath and lonesome bank: Feb. 1895
Far I hear the bugle blow: March 1895
'Tis Spring: come out to ramble: April 1895
Oh, when I was in love with you: May 1895
Along the field as we came by: June (1895?)
When I came last to Ludlow: July 1895
Here the hangman stops his cart: Aug. 1895
Morning up the eastern stair: Sept. 1895
In midnights of November: Oct. 1895
In my own shire, if I were sad: Nov. 1895
Yonder see the morning blink: Dec. 1895
The chestnut casts his flambeaux: Feb. 1896
Wake not for the world-heard thunder: 30 March 1922
Onward led the road again: 10 April 1922
O thou that from thy mansion: 1925